OUTCROPS

OUTCROPS
Terry Gifford

Poems

LITTLEWOOD
1991

for Gill

Published by Littlewood Arc, The Nanholme Centre,
Todmorden, Lancashire OL14 6DA

Printed By Arc & Throstle Press, Todmorden
Typeset by Anne Lister Typesetting, Halifax

ISBN: 0946407 62 2

Cover Design based on a Drawing by Julian Cooper

Acknowledgements are due to the following magazines and journals where some of
these poems previously appeared:–
The Alpine Journal, Cencrastus The Climbing Art (USA), Critical Quarterly,
Climbers' Club Journal, Giant Steps,English in Education, High, Lancaster Festival
Anthologies 1982 and 1985, Pennine Platform, Poetry Nottingham, Poetry Wales,
Reverberations, Staple, Writings '85 (Rotherham Poetry Competition) and York
Open Poetry Competition Anthology 1988. Two poems also appeared in 'The Book of
the Climbing Year', 1988. One poem was published in 'Speak to the Hills', Aberdeen
University Press, 1985.

CONTENTS

Activities in Zone 2-4000

HUTTON ROOF
for David

Coming together like this, warmly,
Through the spitting gale
To your local outcrop, images rise
Towards me as I climb rock
Slippery with slime like fish's scales.
My fingers fit the puddled prints
Like St. Peter's thumb in the haddock,
This white flesh fifteen feet thick
On the boney spine of England.

Surfacing at the summit I see
The gaping mouths of flounders
Piled flat, no longer flapping
On this fossilised beach,
Storm-washed and dipping
Into seas of wet bracken
Where my daughter's red hood
Submerges like a vivid flower
I do not want to lose.

She's unaware that I'm awash
With choices. I do not name
The surface of my thoughts.
You do not ask.
With this we're both at sea,
Swimming amongst the coral,
Sunk for the winter under
This surging of clouds, this wind
That tears at the exposed bedrock.

STASIS

Mist muffles any questions
left between us. Anyway
each droplet in the wood
holds the same answer:

Struggling through wet alders
is too much like
struggling through wet alders
with you again.

Sweating and shivering
against the slope and the drips
I know that nothing new
will be felt or seen today.

Restless jackdaws cackle through the fog,
last icicles melt in grey silence,
another Sunday wastes away from us.
Is this what we've settled for?

BALLOONS

No room in my house today
Holds silence. Children, television,
Unspoken conversations penetrate
The membranes of each room.

Escaping, frankly, in the car
To hear a poet on cassette
I park beside poor pasture
And snipe-holes in wet heather.

To indulge my guilt I drink
The beer for tonight's meal,
Avoiding the glances shot from under
Bunched shoulders of oncoming

Posses of Sunday cyclists
Herding themselves up the hill.
From my bubble I see horses
At Paul Muldoon's Hoy fair.

Red and blue, two balloons
Cross the windscreen, high
And fast, tugging to get free,
Like boxers, from each other,

Only rebounding harder, red and blue
At the ends of what it is that ties them,
Careering straight over the landscapes's
Hedged net of lanes towards

The city. A beech tree bursts,
Turns inside out in a sudden gust.
I shudder, start the car
And roll downhill towards home.

HALLOWE'EN FIRES, BORROWDALE

A black cat walks a wet lane
Under yellow-needled larch skirts,
A bat flickers above flood-fields
Edged with mossed worms of oakroots,
And here at the Celtic year's end
Her voice comes clear in my head,
Straight as a fence post,

A challenge I could be tied to
Like a guy of straw and sisal, burnt
Above broken boughs and old beds
For tunneling towards the core of her, fierce
As a firebrand of red-berried rowan
Blazing against overwhelming powers, tough
Under her skin smooth as a beech trunk.

The red squirrel knows the danger. He
Pauses, listens for evil on the air, then
Returns to his hoardings against winter's worst.
He tunnels for kernels beneath flaming leaves
And yet keeps guard against surface threats.
I need the light of the turnip lantern,
Blazing eyes swinging through the dark.

LAWRENCE IN TRIER

On the coach back the kite cruising
Beside us, turning and turning choices
Of trees on broad wings of ease, shows us
The ragged browns and whites of his breast.

Turning and turning inside the great black
Permanence of Porta Nigra, the Roman gate,
I tell you that inside I'm in turmoil
Thinking of Lawrence's letter to Ernest Weekly
And you, the butterfly on the spiral stairs
In the heart of Trier, Lawrence's Matlock Town
Held in the deep red arms of the valley.

Turning and turning in the streets of Trier
We hunt Lawrence's hotel, letters in our hands.
'I love you because of your chin',
He wrote to Frieda, waiting for her
To join him in these streets of 'pink explosions'.
The vines on his hills 'like angry hedgehogs'
Are each pruned to a heart turning and
Turning with the years on upright stakes.

Brimfull like the shining river, you say
You feel secure staked in our red earth.
It's not strange how I suffer in spite of this,
Turning over choices as I watch you,
Purple shirted and delicate, walking around
The cold black bulk of Porta Nigra.
Certainly our nights snatched here have been
Richly red as a kite turning softly upon
The rising air of a wood. At least Lawrence,
Waiting in Trier, had made his choice.

WHARNCLIFFE CRAG

does not welcome
with an outstretched slope.
Under the railway lines,
through the echoing puddles
and over ankle-wrenching
angular black boulders,
Wharncliffe fights dirty
from the start.

It does not give an inch
to weak, reaching arms
or unhardened hands.
There are no tryouts,
no soft landings,
no resting places
to reassemble
unhardened heads.

It was the nearest crag
to bring you, love,
on our half-day strike.
Somehow the heather
and the silver birches
muted the view
of British Steel's
Stocksbridge Works below.

While the world worked
we climbed warm rock
that left our fingers
stained with Victorian smoke.
You struggled into harness
and fought the unfamiliar
steepness of first climbs,
rising above uncertainty.

The pylons that stepped
over the crag,
monstrously mimicking
its straight hard lines,
seemed to have caught
something in the air
that could not escape
but quietly hummed.

YARNCLIFFE QUARRY

could tell a tale
spin a yarn
                like spiders
across its branches
carried by ants
                up its bush-telegraph aretes
danced by midges
battling with bats
                along the edge of night.
a crepuscular tale
an open secret
                open as a gate
secret as a wood
holding hidden stone
                of magical narratives
latecomers discover ledges
disguised from a grounded view
                at dusk
when the griffins walk
cardinals crack
                night -
fall pipes the goddess in
to her mysterious domain
                the quarry's
cliffe of yarns

SAXON MERMAID

I entered Zennor church uneasily,
Curiosity fighting childhood sermon memories
Mingled with this sense I'd rationally dismiss
Of submitting once again to an upright tower,
These foresquare stones, the judgement
Of this dark door whose latch I choose to lift.

But I stepped into a granite cave of light where
Columns and arches glinted pink and white.
On them rested the familiar form of an upturned
Boat in the roof of barrel vaulting. Spring flowers
Led us in our search for a pagan image
Carved in wood disguised as a seat.

She is hard and dark, the Zennor mermaid,
Defaced by someone's fear of her eyes,
But the swell of her hips, the swirl of grain
In her navel, it's centred depths, and her salty
Low-slung tail of scales still tell what tempted
The chorister down to Pendour Cove to enter sea.

And late that same day I abseiled into a zawn
To stand before a climb called 'Saxon', nervous
Below that towering slab, brittle, steep and black.
Two attempts to unlock its start, then glancing back
There you were, curled on the flowered headland,
Waving, smiling, bright as the Cornish light.

IMBOLC

She stood waiting in her sheepskin
Looking down the long dipping line
Of the black gritstone edge,
The bowl of its back sifting snow
Under a wind from the east quarter.

The sun had probably set
Behind that snow-dark sky.
She had probably missed him
Passing through the sacred rocks
On separate tracks to the high point.

Walking on to keep warm
She remembered the sun orange
On orange bracken last Hallowe'en
When he first showed her
The high cave, its tunnel and balcony,

First whispered that they be Imbolc wed.
Now the nerve of that amulet charmer
Had probably failed. "Walk no further!"
She turned. Panting, he threaded through
Boulders of snow, paused. They walked forwards

To kiss the kiss that binds
But knows the changes of the seasons,
The length of a life.
As their heads parted she smiled,
"How short the shaman has left your hair!"

Two crows passed above, silent,
And she hoped that next year
She would not be here for
The walking apart. They could last,
For all his lateness, beyond the trial.

Now, looking back from a place at the edge
He showed her her head profiled in stone,
Pointed nose and delicate mouth facing west.
Together they ran down towards the tribe where
She would light the great Imbolc fire.

15

ASPENS

nd she came through the trees, slowly,
Touching each slender stem as though
Leaving behind something planted there.

On the far open edge of the wood
Where knee-binding bracken gave way
To the thicket, he stumbled on in.

Closed by these wands she felt safe.
By a lean here, a sway there,
They parted a path she seemed to know.

Missing all paths he bent and tangled.
Pushing forwards he fought saplings
For a future, tripped by dead wood.

Reading the black braille on white bark
And hearing the high song of green
In the leaves she stood sensing her juices.

He wept when she found him, worn out,
Broken, still talking, although later, avoiding
The aspens, he doubted that she had.

ABSEIL

A German word
                    ought to help
order your thoughts
                    in the thin chain
of sling, crab and rusting peg
                    this ancient ring
that anchors you
                    and your partnership
down to earth
                    above
the sucking wet element
                    see
it's surging up the wall
                    again
between your legs
                    trust
the wild bouncing strain
                    don't think
of the thin ring
                    don't drop
off the end
                    into the swelling
sea
                    it wasn't so bad but
will
                    we pull through
together?

DOLPHINARIUM, PHANTASIALAND, COLOGNE

I don't think you quite understood
At the time what happened to me
As I faced upto Phantasialand.
The plastic Brandenburg Gates
Were the first hoop after the turnstile,
The surging roller coaster high
On your list, love. I just found
This need to read under the trees.

I hoped we'd meet half-way
At the two o'clock display of dolphins.
But when, sitting alone, I missed you,
Lost with the German commentary,
My heart went out to the dolphins
And you, as I watched the pool
And the door between whistles.

How they leapt and surged,
Lifting their lives clean
Out of their element
For all to see and grasp
In a gasp what dolphin means:
An underwater force bottled
In a gleaming skin of grey plastic,
A blue pool and a great room
Of alien echoes and faces in tiers.

NORTH HILL TOR

Suddenly the horses started running
Over the green salt marsh,
As though fire swept down
Through crags and trees
Catching at their tails,
Till some invisible force turned them
Full gallop back over creeks.

The wild rhythm of slapped mud
Echoed up to us on the rock
Roped together to a single flake,
All four, a new family
Feeling our way, in turn,
Up the slab's surface,
Unnerved slightly
By whatever was going on.

On top I saw a peregrine
Fly free across the marsh,
Peering down, in control,
Like the small daughter I'd left,
Setting out her ducks and geese
On her bedroom floor.
And here three shelduck lifted
Like flags, black and white
Toys set up for the game.
As my stepdaughter tussled
To untie herself I pointed out
The buzzard slowly circling
And as the rain fell

I was the only one
Who heard the first cuckoo.

WINDGATHER ROCKS

He approached the teeth
of the wind, those
black fangs forced
through soft green gums.

He found a black net
of stone, sagging skeins
billowing back between
anchored aretes

gathering wind,
netting the spiders
climbing across the fine
strands of its web.

He stepped into
its sensuous symmetry
hooked on its edges,
swung from its lips,

and he knew,
even as he savoured
this evening's return to her,
he was caught here for life.

ETIVE TIME

On the third day of rain
Their watches stopped.
Glen Etive time took hold
Of their heads, the way light,
Surreal, red, inside the tent
Seemed to penetrate their brains,
The way the rain drumming
Its mantra on the taut,
Thin, red skin so close
To their eardrums on the ground
Beat the retreat to uneasy sleep.

On the fourth day, although rain stopped
Actually falling as if for the Flood
The sky of mist pressed down
On their prone bodies, a grey weight
Level as the loch, its heavy mirror
Two hundred feet above the slow,
Slow tides. Etive time still held.

On the fifth day a wine-box
Hung from the tree at evening.
Pine-scented smoke rolled from a circle
Of white quartz stones. Heads lifted
To the glen-echoing owl
And midges made forays behind
The ears. Etive time unwound.

On the sixth day breakfast
Pacing the road already burning,
Sweat sweet for bites to the head,
Too light, too hot, too early,
Awaiting the start for the slabs
Surely a source of thermal movement
In the great stone clock of Etive time.

On the seventh day the serpent rested
In Glen Etive under the purple blooms
Of rhododendrons in abandon
As their small white car wound up
Against the rhythm of the river still
Cutting and shaping, feeding and taking,
In the watered clock of rock.
Their lives now sprung from Etive time.

DESCENTS, CALIFORNIA

Always I stayed too long up there,
in too deep, out too far
on the highest places,
turning on those pinnacle points
towards snow, lakes, woods
and whole ranges of colour,
soft High Sierra skylines
of cloud shadowed strata –
red rounded Dana
or the white Minarets.

But the descents were yours
in more than just direction,
or my guilt, or sheer speed
flowing down the dust scree
off Mount Hoffman, then loping along
the last hidden meadow
before jogging round rocks
to May Lake and shouting
your name, echoing
across the still water.

And from Cathedral Peak
reading boulders like chessmen
across grooved glacial slabs
to pick up the trail, panting
but feeling antelope-fit
over the logs of Budd Creek
and sensing the Meadows road
getting closer and closer,
three hours late from my 'solo'
but through darkening trees
calling your name again
and again . . .

You'd brought beer in the car
and wanted no nonsense
like 'The summits are mine
but the descents are yours.'

AUTUMN AMULET

A gale tears across the Fens
The Fen wind turns white sails
The sails drive the windshaft
The windshaft creaks its cogs
Small cogs still turn my wheel
My wheel is driven by phone calls
Your calls crackle across the sea
The sea will turn our tide
Tides rise to your return
Your return will cause a gale

SOMEWHERE ABOVE SWALEDALE

All it needs
is fifteen feet
of weathered rock,
a hole in the ground
without a name
will do
for a winter afternoon
two strangers
and their gear
(your boots are always
in your boot),
a tree
to top-rope from
and whilst the old routine
of ritual 'taking in'
and 'lowering off'
is enacted
for each other
amid laughter, curses,
and mock advice,
something else
is taking place,
not in the sky
exactly,
although
that is what
we speak of
to each other.

'Turn round
at the top
and see that
pink!'

'It's not pink
now, it's yellow.
No, it's green.'

Walking back
we talk
of goats.

MOUNTAIN DULCIMER

'I am on a lonely road and I am travelling,
Looking for something. What can it be?'
Castle Naze hanging in the haze somewhere
Above the lanes leading away from Manchester,
Bursting out as we were from that cloistered
Conference, two Daves and me singing with Joni:

'I want to be strong. I want to live long.
I want to belong to the living.'
First route, last long pull on the pinnacle's
Top edge, singing, strong in just shorts,
Back bare to the sun. At that chill moment
The top block rocked back with me.

'Alive, alive, I want to get up and jive.
I want to have fun, shine like the sun.'
I wanted to get down, breath again on the ground,
Re-start nervous on The Nithin, do The Fly Walk.
And back by the car, Joni's dulcimer strumming
Above fields and farms, we, all three, danced.

AILLADIE, COUNTY CLARE

The fiddler of Doolin was sleeping
But the pub window advertised
'Music Food Drink Crack'.
Out there, in the bright early light,
The Aran islands slept, shifting a little,
Uneasy in a chill Atlantic sea.

Through the green patchwork of cut
And uncut meadows, lanes tacked towards
The stepped white sheets of the hill
Where club-foot ferns crouched in folds and clints
And orchids bristled up through cliff-top tracks.

We were approaching a new crag again,
Sniffing out, as usual, signs of the descent,
Then balanced across cliff-bottom boulders
Reading cracks and corners from a thin book.
Following a ledge leading under a wall
That reared sheer and seductive

Suddenly we stepped on flowers
Sweating under cellophane. 'For Simon'
Said the faded card pinned down
By stones from the crag that killed him
And that we had come to climb.

THE LABYRINTH STONE

Glistened by the bend in the road,
A black boulder of tiny stars,
Its myriad crystals catching low light
Off the sea below the steep hill.

The pilgrims had paused at the sight
Of the sea, then turned to the stone
And its carved maze of circles
On this bend above the Burren.

Waymarker, waymaker, this stone
Was the book of the Burren,
Mapmaker and signmarker for new
Readers of this limestone land.

And as the pilgrims lifted their packs,
Regained their rhythm, they knew now,
Nearing the end of their journey,
That it also had an inner shape.

FROM LUNDY INTO HALLOWE'EN

Surfing downwind from the storm-thrown rock
We slowed towards dusk and Ilfracombe,
A lattice lantern hung high
At a sea-cut door in the coastal walls.
Stilled, we turn in the harbour's lock
To close the centuries we'd lived among.

Driving, clumsily, a car again
We climb past the chip-shops,
Amusements and arcades, half hibernating here,
Recalling before they're unwound by the Devon lanes
The links of Lundy's anchor chains:
Ritual beaching in an open boat,
High winds on orange sunset cliffs,
Pumping water from the well.
Nostalgia riddles us already
Towards the motorway and service-station.

Yet, as we wind down to each Devon village
History giggles alive behind its mask,
Tradition scampers through the streets
In mischief at the doors.
In Porlock we glimpse a pointed hat
Three feet high on a four foot figure,
In Washford whited faces
And much flapping of cloaks.
In Williton pumpkin heads
Swing past the pub,
And in Nether Stowey bulbous masks
Move in a pack with a rubber grin.

Between the creeping miles of ancient banks
And owl-drifted hedgerows
Our headlights flicker past
These old realities resurfacing
Between the dark of the moon
And the wild of the sea.

IN THE MOUNTAINS THEY HAVE A DANCE
Karpathos 1987

In the mountains they have a dance
For every stage of life
For every stage of the festival:
The gathering together,
The stepping down
The track towards the sea,
The night in the cave.

The dancers may change
But the dance is constant
As a candle rising and falling
In the cave of Saint Nicholas,
In whose name the ouzo flows,
Metexa is sipped, hands are joined
In the open circle of sliding steps.

In the mountains they have a dance
To end the dance.
But some villages by the sea
Have forgotten how to close
The circle of a festival
With the last dance, the only dance,
That goes the wrong way round.

In the dance named Peplophorus
With a shudder everywhere,
Young girls in their veils
Danced away from the Turks,
One by one dropping over
The edge of the cliff.
In the mountains they have a dance.

CRETAN WAVES

for Evie

Like a wave on the sea
Rising and falling
To lift it's head and bow
Inward, again and again,
The line of arms linking
Shoulder to shoulder
Lifts and sideslips
In its ancient circle.

It is pulled by a power
Between sea and moon
That turns the dance round a tree
In the village on the mountain.
Steps repeat the tracery
Of foam lace on the shore.
The leader of the line
Flails his white boots in
The fiercest roll of the surf.

And the wave gains length
And the wave gathers speed
And the music of what is happening
Drives bouzoukia and lyre
Towards that moment
Of breathless silence,
That exhausted exhilarated moment:
The afterdance.
It finds its voice
In the old man's parting words:
'God made only one mistake.
He forgot to make us all one nation'.

Next day we wind our way
Up to Aptera,
High on the hill
Above Souda Bay,
To see layered
In stone upon stone
Wave upon wave
Of sea-born settlers,
Invaders, seeders of civil war,
Guardians of this gate to the bay.
Now we look down
On a NATO defence.
Out in the bay
A battleship waits.

So finally we wait
By the surf
For tomorrow's taxi
Back to the airport.
Wave after wave
Of tourists from Europe
Will refill our beds,
Dance in our shoes,
Be bussed each week
To a village in the mountains
For 'The Cretan Experience'.
The wiry old man will preside
Over the dancing
With his wild dignity,
A sparkling eye,
A solo of circling,
A whirl with the women,
And his mad display
Of hanging feet-first from the tree.

Shoulder to shoulder he'll dance
With all nations,
Teaching the steps
And showing their meaning,
Week after week,
Wave after wave.

ON THE BEACH

At night
not long after dark
Giant Loggerhead Turtles
are coming ashore.

We cannot see them
somehow
wherever we wait
however patient we are

however hard we stare
at the surf-caressed sand
for black shapes
staggering slowly

out of the sea.
We have been told
they are digging
their holes and pushing

up piles of sand
to lay their eggs
where they were born
or at least

nearby, in sand
still undisturbed
by the claws
of the Giant Caterpillar.

At daylight
not long after dawn
Giant Caterpillars
are crossing the shore.

We cannot avoid
hearing them
wherever we sit
however patient we are

however hard we stare
at the surf-caressed sand
the black shapes
stagger slowly

almost up to the sea.
We have been told
they are digging
their holes and pushing

up piles of sand
to lay their foundations
where they were born
or at least

nearby, in sand
still undisturbed
by the claws
of other Giant Caterpillars.

THE BULL OF TEXA

I did not see the bull of Texa
Abandoned on its offshore isle.
Defying the final round up
It went wild, the red-haired boatman said.
It was allowed its choice,
The unboatable bull of Texa,
Until, he thought, they shot it,
Salvaging some of their investment.

I did not see the bull of Texa
Startled in the ruined church
As the others did, or said they did,
Soon after we landed on the broken quay.
Trotted off like a bullfight specimen
They said, retreating lean and angry
Into its disturbed domain. Caliban
Or Minotaur, it haunted my island day.

I did not see the bull of Texa
Watching from the centre of his isle
The others on their way back to the boat
Each, like me, now clutching a frail stick.
I had turned the island on its shores,
Found the places where the otters run,
Seen the cliff-ledge falcon nest,
Heard nothing but a sea of sharp bird cries.

I did not see the bull of Texa
Smile, as they said, turning towards the sea
Seeming to prefer his celibate retreat,
His holy byre and his pagan life
That always kept this other race
Well to the edges, backs to the sea,
Never longer than a day. For us
The boatman came at four o'clock.

DIPPER

walks the river bed
wings fluted so the water flows
like a silver wind, a water press
formed by bone and feather,

walks up a boulder into air
clear eyed through both elements,
flying water like the valley wind
yet breath-held above the stream,

bobs ill at ease on nervous springs
hunched as under currents of air,
loyal to this mile for life
yet bank and bed provide no rest,

rolls an eye of neither fish nor beast,
bib washed white as bubbling foam,
fat rock-black body, head brown as earth,
doomed to be dipped in water and air.

WALL

Stone blossoms in the mountains
With lichens, moss and ferns,
Green tying into green like
The art of a dry-stone wall.

Meltwater seepage, serious Spring sun,
And greenslate blocks become
The well-placed rocks of a vertical
Garden that encloses a garden.

What's private, firm and high,
For shutting out and keeping safe,
Has been shifted, bulged and bent
By the root-flower of an oak.

And the surface of the stone
That blooms in these rainy mountains
Gives ledges to the lichens
Which hold minerals for mosses

Where the ferns quietly seed,
Rooting to spring apart, season
By season, the wall of the demesne
Once as secure as this lane.

BAT CHARM

Inside the bat the highest sound
Inside the highest sound an echo
Inside the echo a mountain of meanings
Inside the mountain a wet cave
Inside the wet cave a dry chamber
Inside the dry chamber a grooved roof
Inside the grooved roof a leather pouch
Inside the leather pouch a bat
Inside the bat the highest sound

KATE GIFFORD

My upright grandma bent
Finally from seventy years
Over sink, field and floors,
Died in her apron
On the backroom bed.
As she had bent, fallen, and again
Curled inwards slowly
She stiffened
Against the senility of 'a home'.

The homes her working life had gripped
Were only two, wife and widow.
Her husband's death forced her
From fields of flowers
To the terrace in the town.
In those scrubbed houses
Starched with her iron presence
I always tensed with fear,
Grateful for the chocolate
And the front door, the backward step
To where mistaken wrongdoings
Were natural as growing up.

During a summer stay,
Ten and turbulent,
Sinking into the fantasies
Of the vast feather bed
I was always troubled
By the vagueness of my guilt.
Sunday School, soap and eleven-plus success
Pleased her and my dead grandad,
'Had he been here'.
Always I drew back
From the boney kiss
And its unspoken demands.

Yet talking, nodding, smiling deeply
She held my babies best,
And when we buried her,
Back in the freshly turned
Village soil, I mourned for this
And her unbroken spirit
That even in death demanded
Our long journey
Behind her polished coffin
From street to stubble
And testing Fenland wind.

HILL STRUCTURE

for David Walker Barker

The body of the hill lay open,
Not surgically cut by mechanical digger
And the shotfirer's probe exploring a vein,
Not raw quarried flesh
For the making and remaking
Of arterial motorways pulsing
Their way through the land.

The body of the hill lay open
To the scientist, not the sheep farmer
Who knew the lines of its bones,
Named each of its parts,
Paid the price
Of its high-rainfall pollution
In counts of dead lambs.

The body of the hill lay open
To the scientist reading the photograph,
A map-making X-ray showing
Through a freak filter of Russian radiation
That the huge hips of the earth-figure
Under the geiger-grass were waiting
Their time to start breeding again.

ICE SKATES

Len skated in his youth
along the frozen village river
onto the open waterways
that drain the Fens
like the raised veins on the back
of his eighty-two year old hands.
Leaning into that winter wind
under that grey Fen sky
above those shrinking sheeted floodfields
I see him settling into the rhythm
that will swing him along to Ely.

He sits now by his little coal fire
dispensing old-fashioned opinions like humbugs,
one of the few left along the High Street
with feet firmly set in the ground
of the 1918 British Legion allotments
given to the remnants of the Empire's defenders.
My foothold in that warm and welcoming backroom
always slips away with the talk
of 'coloureds' and 'coons'. I leave again for the city.

Then he gave me his ice skates from the shed,
sleek steel blade rusted rough,
slender wooden platform holed by worm,
great broad screw denied a bite
into a leather heel for half a century.

I sat again and learned
about the field down Parson's Drove
they flooded each February for racing,
about his work as carter to the station,
about a 'pony' of old beer,
and now we steer the talk
across thin ice
so I can tell my son's kids
the life along the edge of Len's old skates.

FISHFACE

He knew they had to be passed
Like passing a dog
That smells your fear.

Gary's gang smelled his
And they guarded this street
Into which his family had moved

Gary made the teams
And the mischief
For his scrawny band of littluns.

'Oi! Fishface!'
He kept walking
But mentally he froze.

He knew he had no safe reply.
They had him hooked
And played him down their line.

Now he could not change.
His ears moved like gills
On the face that swam towards him

Every morning in the mirror.

MRS RIDGEON'S GARDEN

It was not his father's obvious delight,
It was not the fusty smell of stored apples,
It was not even the eight year old's pride
At cycling with dad's forgotten sandwiches
To 'the old lady's' as it was called at home.

It was the stark formality he entered uneasily
Between clipped high hedges, over even gravel,
Beside turf-trimmed weedless borders, he remembered,
And the slowly growing sense that his father's
Mower, shears, hard-grained hands had shaped

This powerful message for the owner, who,
He slowly realised, also owned his dad.

"A FIELD NEAR VERNHAM DENE"
by Frances St. Clair Miller

Rising from the reedbed
she looked uneasily around:

only the terns shrieking,
and a cutting sea wind

bending the grassheads towards
her, snatching at her sketchbook

in its wild rushes. She held on.
No-one there. She relaxed again.

Always when she broke from
the reverie of drawing, this guilt,

and always in this moment
she saw her real subject

rising through the surface
of the patterns on paper.

But her eldest son was not
here, except in the crossed lines

of her study, the wild shrieks
of the terns and the cutting wind.

DEEPDALE CAMP

between the drumlins' soft breasts
we lay back
replete as the resting turf
and let night come
to the rattle of beck boulders
and conversation
stilled by flares of shooting stars
entranced by arches of orbit
silent moments of fiery extinction.

silent next morning
the sheep suffered the crow
at its empty eye-sockets
stirring a leg only
as we passed.

THE WRECK

Two grey-haired hitchhikers
Had started walking the long road
That leads to the cliff-top,
The war memorial and the sea.

The tall wife bent into our car,
Bunched with her husband in the back.
Their German accents gave us guesses
At the story they had to tell.

They came to find his father's grave
In the shifting seas below
The crumbling cliffs at the Mull of Oa.
We came to find that this year's nest

Of newborn choughs had shifted
From the cave-dark of arched sea-stack
To a cleft outside this monumental stone,
Wrecked here between sea and shore.

Doubling for a friend, his father drowned
In the fog-dark of a Christmas Eve,
Taking herrings from Tarbert in 1924.
Our guilt had assumed it was the war.

We drove them across the island to a church,
Now a museum, where a chart of wrecks
Was photographed as if they'd found
At last, a gravestone for the 'Hoheluft'.

Young black birds now lift from the cliff
Where on that night the islanders stood
Helpless, like us, to do or say
The things that save or heal.

THE ELTERWATER OTTERS

In dull dawn light I creep
Across the creaking boards, unlock
The heavy hostel door and hunt
The Elterwater otters once again.

Behind me my children sleep alone
Snug as badgers in their bunks,
If they don't wake. In the midge-soft
Heavy morning it's misty across the meadow.

Tensed for what's behind and what's
Before, swiftly but softly I tread
Gravel by the river. Greenslates glisten
Clear as pennies in a wishing-well.

I watch the dipper underwater,
Its needle head sewing together
The seams of the river as I pass.
Hoping they're still not stirring

Behind me, I stare far downstream
For playful splashes round the rocks
In the shallows and suddenly I'm tripped
By a net of tree roots at my feet.

It must have been as I reached the lake,
Saw the kingfisher dive, flash that blue
Fluorescence of oil in the marsh mud,
That they found my bed was empty.

It must have been as I saw that 'fish'
Paddling along the bed of the lake,
Large as a black log just below me,
That they began to hunt the hostel.

HURRICANE HITS THE GOGS

Gogmagog,
My first hill,
White above the Fen soil
My father's family all worked.

First woodland
Of first expeditions
Scouting beyond the Roman Road
Into the pagan legends of the wood.

Gog and Magog,
Survivor giants living
Within the hidden leaf-dark
Double dyche of Wandlebury Ring.

Light has broken through the wood.
Dead beeches point the path
Of a wind tearing
North-east.

Circles of roots stand upright and white.
My father points to fibrous nets
Holding tiles of chalk –
'No tap-root',

Points to the stain in each sawn core:
'Beech-bark disease' already lay
Within the growth rings
Of the Gogs.

ZINAL ROTHORN

for John Driskell

Whilst Zinal slept
We moved upon the mountain,

First by torchlight on moraine
Then dawnlight on ice until

Sunlight fired first peaks,
Caught our breath in the sharp

Thin air that distilled
My first start, first season.

It was to be your last.
Strange, that we've both lost

The photographs, as though
Memory through the whisky glass

Between us, years after
Your first illness, was stronger

Years after we moved together
Step in step upon the mountain.

WILDSPITZ 1972

'Incompetence was rife' – Richard Gilbert, 1989

Everyone and their grandma
Hustled for the highest point
And the queues strung back
Between summits and below
The icy ramp of bucket steps
Stamped up the Mitterkar Joch.

Grandma wore a headscarf
And a woollen skirt. It was
An Austrian family holiday
Hiking hut to hut. For us
It was a helmet job, hard men
In the making, moleskins and smocks.

But two steps down the ramp
A crampon came free. I went
Sledging on my sac, unable to roll over
Amongst glacier cream, sweets, shouts.
Nick thought I was glissading
And leapt off behind me

Whooping past the cursing guides.

MARGINAL

This, then, is the backside of England
Paraded past the window of every passing train.
The last of the terraces, the latest of the tenements,
'150 PEOPLE LIVE HERE' is painted near St Pancras.
Cars, long since dead, pile up on the edge
Of every English town. And even the green fields
Of England run to waste at the railway
In scraps of linking wilderness, densely overgrown,
Derelict, forgotten, self-seeding, essential
To survival for its wild intimates: foxes and shrews,
Butterflies and children, whose secret tracks
Criss-cross this marginal breathing space.

Scotland sells its mountains to the English (and the Dutch).
Wales markets its moorlands, Ireland worships its bogs.
England simply turns its back on these scabs of scrub and mere,
Fastnesses fenced off from the mind that nonetheless knows
It needs parks and trees and paths and something
That is called, in the papers at St Pancras, 'The Green Vote'.

ACTIVITIES IN ZONE 2-4000

(I)

EVENING WALL, LINING CRAG
(for W. Heaton Cooper, mountain painter)

Fingers are fine brushes
for dipping into wet dabs
of mosses blobbed on the palette
below the canvas of the crag.

Feet are the pointed ends
of sharp pencils, shaped
for toning strokes across
the grain of the crag.

Eyes trace the steady growth
of the composition, the length
and proportion of the line
on the page of the crag.

Sun holds the source
of shadow for the painter
and delight in the evening
of life amongst the crags.

(II)

LINES LEFT UPON A SEAT BESIDE THE BRIDGE INN, CALVER, THE AUTHOR HAVING ASCENDED BASLOW EDGE UPON THE SUNNY SUNDAY MORNING OF THE THIRTY-FIRST OF MAY, NINETEEN HUNDRED AND EIGHTY SEVEN.

(for W. Wordsworth, guidebook writer)

After the starling kids
screamed out of the car park
a black pack of jackdaws descends,
fearless and fully fledged
from the deepest cracks
I've been climbing just now.

They bounce for the bits,
slightly uncertain about walking
or flying between outlying crisps.
Upright and innocent they rush
bullying about their new playground,
still a little pale under
their black school caps,
but who dare doubt the look
from that beaked yellow eye?

Below soaring young jackdaws
and men's bright balsa planes
there's a delicate climb up
a wall of remarkable rock,
a frail flake of gritstone
curves up into a hole hung
only for outstretched fingers to feel.
It is named by some youth
'Death to Khomeini'.

ROCCA DI PERTI

for John Ruskin, who wrote in 1870: "And do we dream that by carving fonts and fitting pillars in His honour – we shall obtain pardon for the dishonour done to the hills and streams by which He appointed our dwelling place?"

They were cutting the mountain
into pats of butter,
great pale blocks,
unmelted even in this heat,
left on a shelf
above the shimmering valley.

Out of the natural tumble
of rounded rocks and bushes
they'd cut a box
into this living shoulder
with clean scalpel blades.

I had to touch its walls
to believe its smoothness,
finger the slicing of pink crystals
sparkling from the granite whiteness,
hear, in the evening stillness,
the breaking of atoms
inside this gentle mountain
from which basilicas are built.

EASTERN ARETE OF NANTLLE Y GARN

(for Mrs. Evelyn Jones, B & B)

He had cleared stones, Mr. Jones,
By hand, bending and lifting,
A hard crop for a sheepfarmer.
He had planted turnips for feed
When we returned two years later
Over the pass to Drws-y-Coed.
There was the good shepherd with
Binoculars watching rams at the ewes.

Through his glasses he watched walls
On the skyline of Nantlle y Garn.
He maintained them by hand,
Bending and lifting stones tumbled
By hill-walkers ticking the summits
Of Wales. But much harder work
Was the crop from Chernobyl,
Decreed as the slaughter of lambs.

Yes, we could climb if we must
On his arete up to the skyline.
(And bold work by hand and head
It's the best of the crop for 1905
Which Haskett-Smith unveiled in
'Twixt Snowdon And The Sea')
Mrs. Jones looked up from Gill to the ridge
And made us an offer of room at the inn.

BORROWDALE EVOLUTION

(for Ian Lonsdale, climber)

And when they turned at last
In the Jaws of Borrowdale and cried
'After the whale, Save the Saxifrage!'
The fenced paths were white stairways
Onto purple fells fertilised for perfection,
Climbing crags were chalk polished
And made safe with BMC bolts,

Fields farmed rare species
Of nearly lost sheep behind
Electric fences sheathed
In Leisure Park green.

And in the Leisure Park office
After many meetings,
Consternations of conferences,
The committee came up with
The Borrowdale Crag Plan:

Upper Falcon Crag to the ornithological interest,
Beth's Buttress to the botanist, refurbishing the ferns,
Castle Crags to the photographer – National View 5003,
Nitting Haws to the scrambler whose guidebook made history,
Shepherd's Crag to the climber who has coughed up the fee.

Now the climber with her National Certificate
Never envies the ornithologist his Borrowdale permit,
And the windsurfer displaying her Derwentwater Disc
Never speaks to the botanist with his SSSIC.
But sometimes a walker with Self-leadership Grade 3
Applies for a day on the Ecological Trail
In triplicate, for next year, if the geiger count is clear.

NOTES

Yarncliffe Quarry   contains the names of five rock-climbs on this crag.

Imbolc,   1 February, was one of the quarter days of the Celtic calendar. On this day a trial marriage could be made by a couple walking towards each other and kissing. This could be broken a year later by walking apart.

Mountain Dulcimer   is the instrument played by Joni Mitchell to accompany the song quoted here from her *Blue* LP.

Ailladie, County Clare   begins with a reference to the village which is famous as the centre of traditional music in the west of Ireland and echoes Yeats' *Fiddler of Dooney*.

The Bull of Texa   lived on this deserted island, a mile long and a quarter wide, off the south coast of the Hebridian isle of Islay.

Hurricane Hits the Gogs   is located on the Gogmagog chalk hills south of Cambridge where the neolithic earthworks of Wandlebury Ring have been overgrown with beeches.

Zinalrothorn   is an Alpine peak above the village of Zinal in Switzerland.

Activities in Zone 2-4000   refers to the contours indicating upland areas in Britain.

Borrowdale Evolution   was commissioned by Ian Lonsdale for his contribution to the 1987 *Crags and Awareness* conference in Ambleside. The BMC is the British Mountaineering Council, the representative body of the sport. An SSSI is a Nature Conservancy Council designated Site of Special Scientific Interest. This poem began life as a satire.

TERRY GIFFORD was born in Cambridge in 1946 and is Senior Lecturer in English at Bretton Hall College. He has published books on Ted Hughes, teaching A level English and teaching poetry writing. Organiser of the annual International Festival of Mountaineering Literature, he writes regularly for the climbing magazines and is poetry editor for *High*. Terry Gifford has run residential courses on writing and climbing, lectured on mountaineering literature, and is currently researching notions of nature in contemporary poetry whilst preparing a forthcoming book on John Muir. His first collection, *The Stone Spiral*, is available from Littlewood Arc and a slide-illustrated performance of his poem sequence *Ten Letters To John Muir* can be arranged through Burbage Books, 56 Conduit Rd, Sheffield S10 1EW (0742 668813). *Ten Letters To John Muir* has raised over £400 for the John Muir Trust's protection of wilderness in Scotland.

8020